DEDICATION

To all the mothers and daughters of this generation and beyond.

"And I will bring the blind by a way that they knew not; I will lead them in paths that they have not known: I will make darkness light before them, and crooked things straight. These things will I do to them, and not forsake them."

Isaiah 42:16

By the Brightness of the day! And the night when it is still!- Thy Lord has not forsaken thee, nor is he displeased. And surely the latter state is better for thee than the former. And soon will thy Lord give thee so that thou wilt be well pleased. Did He not find thee an orphan and give (thee) shelter? And find thee groping, so He showed the way?

Al Duha 93:1-7

NOTE TO READERS

This publication is sold with the understanding that it is not meant to offer or replace medical or psychological advice. Moreover, the general situations described in this book may not apply to your particular circumstances. Therefore, no medical or mental health action in this book should be taken without seeking the advice or counsel of trained medical or mental health professionals. This book is not intended to diagnose, prescribe or be a substitute for physician advice or otherwise.

Mothers & Daughters

A Self-Help and Best Practices Guide for African American Mothers and Their Daughters

Dr. Toni S. Muhammad

Mothers & Daughters: A Self-Help and Best Practices Guide for African American Mothers and Their Daughters
By Toni Sims Muhammad. Contributors: Tynetta Hill Muhammad, Ava Hill Muhammad, Marva Muhammad, Jacqueline Dennis, Nisa Islam Muhammad and Majidah Muhammad

Published in the United States by:
Vanguard Educational Services Academic Press, PO Box 77875, Greensboro, NC 27417

Copyright © 2014 Vanguard Educational Services Academic Press. All rights reserved. No part of this publication may be used or reproduced in any manner whatsoever without the written permission of the Publisher. Printed in the United States of America. Contact us at Vanguard Educational Services Academic Press, vangaurdedsrv@gmail.com.

ISBN: 10: 0985759224
ISBN-13: 978-0985759223

ACKNOWLEDGMENTS

I would like to express sincere gratitude to my family, colleagues and friends for providing me with helpful insights, material and ideas in Mothers & Daughters. I would like to thank my daughters, Tynetta and Ava, who impress me more and more everyday, even more than they realize. Thank you for beginning this journey with me. I am eternally grateful to be the vessel for your entry into this world. I would also like to thank my sons, Amir and Kaeed, whose lives are daily reminders for why this work is so important. I would like to thank my husband, Tarik, whose incredulous insights have guided me through the last few years of parenting our children; but most particularly our daughters. In addition, I would like to thank all of the girls and women who have made a significant impact on my life. The lessons I learned from them have sustained me and reinforced values that make me the person I am today. Here is a partial list of their names, Tempie (mom), Matilda (great-grand) Sarah (muddear), Gussie (grand mom), Matilda (Tee), Joyce Ann, Angelafaye, Dr. Danita, Dionne, Robertine, Erica, Angelique, Marva, Ms. Strickland, Ms. Brown, Ms. Brass, Ms. Cole, Ms. Rambo, Suszanne, Tamiko, Gertrude, Lolita, Loleatha, Odetta, Corliss, Celesia, LaShonda, Tara, Bridgett, Melanie, Dr. Jackie, Mendez, Dr. Rhonda and Felicia. Finally, I wish to express my most sincere and heartfelt thanks to the Honorable Minister Louis Farrakhan for bringing me to the MGT-GCC class – a class that makes me a girl at heart, forever.

Dr. Toni

CONTENTS

Acknowledgments — v

Introduction — 1

Basic Girl Skills

1. Personal Hygiene — 11
2. Dressing the Part — 29
3. Exercise & Physical Fitness — 37
4. "ME" Time — 53
5. Talking With Parents — 61
6. Self-Esteem — 69
7. Finances & Money — 81
8. Friends & Associates — 87
9. School — 93
10. Around the House Life Skills — 99

50 Tips for Mothers — 109

50 Tips for Daughters — 142

INTRODUCTION

Mothers and Daughters begin as an after thought for me during the process of rearing my two daughters. Sometimes it seems easy and I have it all figured out and others times I am frustrated banging my head against the wall like so many mothers (and fathers) of daughters. However, rearing a daughter for many mothers is especially challenging in today's world.

Degenerative and culturally degrading mass media images, rap music and videos, drugs, sexuality, disease, failing public education systems, poor nutrition and eating habits, declining physical fitness, provocative fashion and styles all bring thoughts of fear, horror and downright panic to mind. It is any wonder that girls survive the growing up process at all let alone become productive functional adults. Even after they become young adults and have children, many women may not have gained sufficient knowledge regarding rearing their daughter(s). What do I teach them/how do I help them develop the essential ways to grow into cultured, civilized women? Many parents' desire assistance and guidance with the challenges of parenting. Some parents recognize that there is a need for improvement in their child rearing skills but do not have the knowledge, resources and support to help their children so that they do not have to experience the trials and errors of life. We curse each generation when we do not have the opportunity to study and improve upon the previous generation. Our goal as parents should be as the expression many of us heard growing up, "we want you to do (be) better than us." Parents want their children to escape and avoid the pitfalls they experienced growing up and this guide seeks to assist them.

Moreover, there is the unfortunate dilemma happening right before many mothers (and fathers) eyes, especially African Americans ...young black and female wondering the "streets" day and night, getting caught up in clandestine relationships with men (usually 10 years their senior) without any guidance or direction. Girls dancing provocatively on YouTube for attention and money. When you drive down the road in economically deprived neighborhoods, it is common to pass teenage girls outside at all times of the night. Many of us are afraid to approach them, and if we do approach them, we may not know what to do or say. Some of our girls may feel that they are alone in this world (or so they have been convinced) and how can "you" convince them any different.

As a black woman, it not only makes me want to holler, it gives me grief, makes me cry, and I dare to say that it even keeps me up at nights. Ultimately, all I want to do is save them. Save them from this world full of traps. In the black community and throughout this society, black girls especially those without the "strong super mom black woman" (or even a virulent father) fall into trap upon trap, upon trap. Once they are caught, they may never escape.

Yet, so many African American mothers are unclear about how to take a direct role and responsibility for teaching their daughters what they need to know in order for them to grow into womanhood. Many are confused themselves about what to do and some shy away from the process because of fear that they will fail. What many African American mothers must do is come together and form community girl-rearing cores so that sisters, colleagues, mothers and female cohorts can reverse another detrimental trend affecting our ability to rear our daughters - the fact that the black female marriage rate is only 28% percent, which may mean a 4.5 greater risk of poverty for African American children brought up in single-female headed households. Another duplicitous question parallel to this statistic is - what about the importance and role of the African American male in the rearing (and protection) of their daughters? Many social scientist stress that black men must be involved in the rearing of their sons, but African American girls need fathers too. Far too often black girls are left totally un-nurtured, unprotected, and vulnerable to every "thing" that creeps and crawls throughout their communities. In fact studies show that upon release from incarceration, many males convicted of a sexual offense struggle to find a home and this may lead to their settlement (homeless in parks, near schools, substandard housing) in poorer, urban and even crowded areas, i.e., many African American communities.

As I worked in the grassroots, I begin to develop programs and initiatives to assist our African American mothers and their daughters to overcome obstacles affecting their education and empowerment. Some of these programs have inspired this book.

I asked my daughters, colleagues, friends and relatives to share a few insights, ideas, experiences and knowledge about the topics in this book. We hope that this is a start for mothers (fathers too) and their daughters.

Toni Sims Muhammad

Toni Sims Muhammad

Basic Girl Skills

Mothers & Daughters

"A Nation Can Rise No Higher Than Its Woman."

The Honorable Minister Louis Farrakhan

CHAPTER 1
PERSONAL HYGIENE

The truest indicator of how you feel about yourself is how well you take care of your body, more specifically your personal hygiene. Hygiene care includes hands, feet, hair, ears, neck, genital area and body fluid perspiration. Many young girls do not receive clear or direct instruction about how to take care of these matters and unfortunately, many women have had to experiment on their own or learn as they grow. It is important that our girls be given proper information; instruction and guidance for personal hygiene and here are some suggestions:

Hands

Wash your hands often when you are away from home. Always wash your hands as soon as you return home. Wash hands by using soap, and if possible use a small manicure brush to loosen soil. Consider pouring a little alcohol on the brush to scrub under fingernails and hands. Dry hands with a clean towel and always moisturize.

An ounce of prevention is a pound of cure. So, when out, carry a small purse with your own personal ink pen. This eliminates having to use other's pens. In addition, carry hand sanitizer just in case you have to shake someone hand or touch objects for public use. Use paper towel or toilet tissue in bathrooms to open doors, turn on faucets and open and close stall doors. If no paper towels are available upon exiting the bathroom, use tissue or even an elbow, where feasible.

Never sit your purse on bathroom floors, find somewhere to hang it up.

Feet

Pedicures can be great and easily done at home. This is

also a fun activity for mothers and daughters to do together. If you do not have a SPA Tub, purchase a plastic dishpan for a couple of dollars, if you can.

Get everything you will need (also just in case you need to get up): slip on shoes, a towel, lotion, something to read, water, etc. Pour in some warm to hot water. Be mindful of the temperature. Place feet in the water. Add soak additives to help with the removal of rough skin. Use gentle moisturizers to put moisture back in and aloe vera gel and vitamin E as a healing agent for the skin. Always discard used water when done, wash the tub/pan with a mild cleaning agent and let the tub/pan dry out for next use.

Hair

Depending on hairstyle and texture, hair can be washed daily, every other day or weekly. Permed hair can be washed weekly or bi-weekly, depending on the weather and activity. Consult a stylist for more care instructions about permed hair. Natural hairstyles can be washed daily or every other day depending on types of hair, care products used to moisturize it, the weather, and your level and types of physical activity. Here are some other tips about styling hair:

- Wearing hats on your head for prolonged periods may stunt hair growth.
- Ponytails may cause headaches, neck tension and hair loss if worn over prolonged periods.
- Hair should be combed or style with fingers to fit your face, round, oval, long. Check out hair magazines for models and styles to see what works for you.
- Scarves make for attractive hairpieces and can create another dimension for outfits.

Face

Wash your face first thing in the morning and before bed. People may hug and kiss your face throughout the day so cleansing before bed is especially a good habit. Use a gentle perfume free soap, lather in hands, and then gently apply to face by lightly using fingertips and creating a circular motion. Do not use fingernails. Do not scrub your face. Cup water in your hands and rinse off. Be sure to remove all soap or face cleanser. Blot dry, do not rub dry.

Witch Hazel is a good alternative to alcohol for cleaning your face. Use gentle moisturizers such as aloe vera gel and vitamin E to heal scars and put moisture back in skin. Do not attempt to burst (pop) pimples, it will leave a scar. Instead, drink more water, usually half your body weight in ounces. If you weigh 100 pound, then drinking at least 50 ounces of water a day may help your digestive process and pores cleanse themselves. The more water you drink the better.

Keep hair away from face because oils from hair may also clog the pores. Modify food choices such as candy, sodas and other high synthetic sugar choices may help with reducing breakouts and flare up.

Teeth

Rinse your mouth with water before brushing your teeth especially when you have just finished eating. Brush your teeth at least twice a day. Use toothpaste as an agent to aid in cleansing your teeth. Use floss to clean between teeth and mouthwash or rinse. If eating out, make it a habit to rinse the mouth after you eat, even if using just plain water. Swish the water back and forth using your tongue to touch every surface of your teeth and gums. Always check your teeth for food particles on or stuck between them. If so, strong swishing may help to dislodge.

Ears/Neck/Shoulders

Use alcohol on cotton swabs/balls to cleanse neck areas and shoulders, behind ears. The amount of dirt left behind, even after showering, is amazing. In addition, cleansing these areas can be done easily with this method inside the shower. Wet your towel with water and apply soap to towel, wash over areas and rinse off. Then use a cap full of alcohol on the towel and wipe over ears, neck and shoulders. Be sure to rinse off again. Use gentle moisturizers such as aloe vera gel and vitamin E to put moisture back in skin.

Underwear (Genital Areas)

A key to a healthy genital area is your underwear. Often times this is overlooked as essential. Of course, cleansing is just as important, but next in line is underwear. Underwear must be clean, stain free and odor free. Underwear should be changed once a day, twice a day if you perspire excessively. Light grooming of pubic hair helps with perspiration during warm/hot weather. Be careful with grooming instruments – if you are not sure, ask your mom or family doctor about the best way to groom pubic hair. Cotton underwear is best. Underwear should be comfortable, not tight around the thighs or causing discomfort.

Some tips: (to avoid severe irritation and allergic reactions)
- ❖ Always wash your hands (in the shower or bath) first, before touching your genitals, especially if you have fingernails. Be mindful that skin in the genital area is very delicate and sensitive so be careful not to scratch or cut yourself.
- ❖ Do not use soap on your genitals. Lather soap in your hands then carefully wash the genital areas immediately. Do not attempt to wash inside yourself.
- ❖ When showering, keep a cleansing bottle handy just in case you want to rinse genitals more thoroughly.
- ❖ Do not put powder in your underwear.
- ❖ Do not put lotions close to genital areas.

❖ Do not spray/splash perfumes, body sprays, colognes, alcohol or peroxide near or on genitals.

To feel refreshed, simply spray or put perfume/cologne on a cotton swab or cotton ball and gently pat or rub in areas such as the small of back (lower back, slightly above bottom), the waistline area, hip area, behind knees, elbow, neck line, back of upper thigh, and/or elbow. Pay attention to any skin reactions that may occur. Discontinue using any product that causes an allergic or uncomfortable reaction.

Perspiration

If possible, girls should wear deodorant rather than antiperspirant. Some mass media images portray that sweating is not good or that it is bad for us. This is far from the truth. Sweating is good for us. It is a sign of a healthy cleansing system. Our girls must be encouraged to find activities or ways to sweat, especially when not involved in sports and outdoor activities. We must encourage physical activity and teach them the proper use of deodorant. To this end, when we sweat, especially when it is warm/hot weather we must shower daily and twice if necessary. When it is cool weather, girls should shower daily (at least once every 24 hours). Showering before bed is encouraged as it will relax the body for sleep. Showering in the morning can provide the pick me up to get your day started.

Girls should check clothing for perspiration smells and stains. Apply detergent or some other cleaning agent (not bleach) prior to washing, to get rid of smells. Consider adding vinegar or other cleaning agent to your laundry for strong odors. Underwear should also be free of smells and odors after washing. If not, adjust the amount of detergent used to wash them and re-wash. Give attention to detergent instructions.

Baths & Showers

Shower daily and take a tub bath at least 3 times a month. Bath water should be clear and free from perfumes and dyes including soaps that contain harsh chemicals. Be careful submerging your bottom in a tub. Bubble baths and soaps may be too harsh for your delicate areas. If you do use soap, use soap that is dye free, chemical free and additive free. To do some extra hygiene cleansing add 1 cup of vinegar to your bath water. Be sure to talk to your doctor for follow-up and additional suggestions or instructions. For more great tips on the use of vinegar visit: http://vinegartips.com/

Tip: Always use a hand towel for shower and bath.
When you exit the bath, it is very refreshing to take a quick 3 -5 minute shower to wash off any sediment from the bath. Pat dry. Consider adding alcohol to your washcloth while in the shower. This can be a very effective cleansing regimen for armpits and feet, which accumulate excessive amount of oils and dirt from deodorant, lotions, etc.

Menstrual Cycle
Marva Muhammad
Use a calendar (pocket or purse size) to jot down when cycle begins/ends. There are also several Apps for keeping track of your menstruation - Check one out at http://www.freemenstrualcalendar.com/. A shower should be taken twice a day during heavy days. Sanitary napkins are recommended and should be changed every 2-3 hours during the day. Extra pads should be kept on your person as well as an extra pair of underwear in case of an accident. Heavily soiled underwear should be

washed immediately and disposed of when unable to come clean. Drink lots of water as this will ensure you do not dehydrate during your menstrual cycle/period.

Use the calendar to mark the 1st and the last day of your period. Then count 21 or 28 days after the last day. Usually that is the 1st or around the first day of your period. This method of calculating your cycle helps when you have cramps or bloating. By doing this, you can start preparing to take special care of yourself.

Organizing Your Personal Space

The key to knowing where everything is to put everything in its own place. Create a space in your room or area that is just for you and your personal items.

- ❖ Keep socks, underwear, bras and other undergarments in a space all their own.
- ❖ Fold t-shirts, sweaters, and sweatshirts and place on a shelf. Also, fold jeans. Hanging can spoil shape.
- ❖ Hang dress pants/slack, dresses, jackets/blazers and specialty items in your closet.
- ❖ Hang all items that you hate to iron every time you wear them, hang them immediately after wearing.

Remember some items can be worn more than once if they are not soiled during regular wear. These items include sweaters, jeans, jackets, and coats. Do wash or dry clean once soiled.

❖ To prevent shrinking, some clothes are best dried placed over a door or by hanging up.

Reminder

Organize your purse or a backpack to contain the following:

- ❖ 1 Lotion
- ❖ 1 Hand sanitizer
- ❖ 1 Sanitary napkin/pad
- ❖ Lip balm/gloss
- ❖ 1 small/comb and brush
- ❖ Identification

Talk Back:

Rate your areas of hygiene you feel *most* comfortable and confident about your knowledge? Rate your comfort on a scale of 1 to 5, with five being the highest and one being the lowest.

Categories:

Hair	1. _____
Menses	2. _____
Teeth	3. _____
Hands	4. _____
Feet	5. _____
Face	6. _____
Perspiration	7. _____
Personal Space	8. _____
Underwear	9. _____
Bath & Showers	10. _____

To improve in areas where you desire greater confidence and knowledge consider additional research and reading about at least three areas, and of course, increase your practice of hygiene.

Write what you read below:

Title: _____

By: _____

Is it a...
_____ Book   or
_____ Magazine/Internet Article

What was it about? (check one)

_____Hair   _____Menses   _____Teeth

_____Face   _____Feet   _____Hands

_____Underwear   _____Bath & Showers

_____ Perspiration   _____ Personal Space

_____Other _____

Write what you read below:

Title: _____

By: _____

Is it a...
_____ Book   or
_____ Magazine/Internet Article

What was it about? (check one)

_____Hair   _____Menses   _____Teeth

_____Face   _____Feet   _____Hands

_____Underwear   _____Bath & Showers

_____ Perspiration   _____ Personal Space

_____Other _____

Write what you read below:

Title: _____

By: _____

Is it a...
_____ Book   or
_____ Magazine/Internet Article

What was it about? (check one)

_____Hair   _____Menses   _____Teeth

_____Face   _____Feet   _____Hands

_____Underwear   _____Bath & Showers

_____ Perspiration   _____ Personal Space

_____Other _____

Above all else, guard your heart, for it is the wellspring of life."
(Proverbs 4:23)

"There is in this world no greater force than the force of a man/woman determined to rise".
~Anonymous

"Where there are no decent women, there are no descent men."
The Most Honorable Elijah Muhammad

"Phenomenal Woman, That's me."
Maya Angelou

CHAPTER 2
DRESSING THE PART

A Girls Perspective
Tynetta Muhammad

Wear clothes and shoes that provide comfort and fashion appeal. Color coordinate to the extent possible. While there are no rules for color wear, but some good practices are to wear dark colors in the fall/winter and light colors in the spring/summer. Try different colors, prints and styles to see what looks good on you. Your clothes should "fit" your body type. Body types tend to be thin, petite, tall, curvy, and full figure. Look at your mother, grandmothers and aunts because this will give you an idea of future body shape possibilities.

Some simple body types/fabric rules to consider for looking your best:

- *Thin:* jeans, cotton
- *Petite:* polyester blends
- *Tall*: linen, cotton
- *Curvy*: cotton, polyester blends
- *Full*: silks, rayon

Google: fabrics and body shape type for more on this topic.

One of my favorite websites is:
http://www.shopwiki.com/wiki/Figure-flattering+Clothes+for+Women

Loose fitting is best. Soft fabrics such as cottons are cool and fun for easy movement.

Shopping

Shop at thrift stores if possible. Many times, you will find some great deals; designer brands and the clothes will wear like new. My mom and I thrift shop frequently and we also bargain hunt. Just be sure to wash before you wear.

Washing/Cleaning

Use vinegar to clean white that have discoloration. Be careful with bleach especially if using around non-white clothing. Separate colors by fabric type, size and style (t-shirt, dress, slacks, jeans, dress shirt, sweater) and wash according to instructions.

As you get older, you may want to try to impress others and look nice in the eyes of others but you must remember that fashion is a way of expressing yourself! You can send a message with your clothes without even opening your mouth. So always, dress in clothes that flatter you and make people want to respect you.

People will try to read you through your clothes choice before they meet you, so let them be a reflection of your beautiful, true inner self, a girl whose smart, stylish, and knows her worth in God's eyes!

Ask yourself, what message do you want people to think of when they see you in your clothes? Do you want your clothes to say you are a beautiful girl who deserves respect? I am sure you do, so here are my own stylin' tips:

- Try taking clothes from each style, and do not let anyone stereotype you.
- Have fun.
- Surprise people! Get something new that POPS and is totally YOU! Whether it be bright red leggings under a skirt, leg warmers, fingerless gloves, bangle bracelets, a pink ball cap, or a bright yellow purse, make your outfit totally YOUnique.
- You are yourself, and not anyone else! Wear what you feel comfortable in. People cannot force you to do anything. Only you can choose!
- Do not rebel from your parents. They know best. Sometimes it is hard to tell if you are dressing too maturely -- your parents should know if you are dressing in an inappropriate way.
- Never show too much skin. It just does not work.
- Do not wear tight fitting jeans. Jean fabric is not flexible and may cause health problems.

Parents may feel that teenagers often wear clothes that they cannot stand. In their eyes, many teens' outfits make them look odd, clownish, grungy, too sexy, or downright scary. However, the old adage, "Don't judge a book by its cover," is especially true with teens. A nice, kind teen can be hiding underneath an unusual outfit. You job as a teenager is to find your inner qualities and focus on who you are and people will not judge you by what you wear. Fashions and fads come and go, and you are bound to experiment with them. Show your parents that you love and validate them even when your style differs completely from their tastes.

Daughter to Mothers...

There is much more to your teenager than how she dresses. Is she happy? Is she doing well in school? Does she treat people with respect? Does she have healthy hobbies and interests? Is she staying out of trouble? If she's doing relatively well overall, then her outfit is a minor issue - perhaps even a non-issue.

Now back to my girls...

They might think that what you wear endangers you or causes

you to miss opportunities, like getting an opportunity that you really want, but you must try to understand where this concern comes from. Just remember to do so calmly and in the most non-judgmental manner possible. However, you should know that we live in a hyper-sexual/over-sexual society. Most advertisements, movies, music television shows and even cartoons contain an extraordinary quantity of sex. And guess who's watching and listening: we are. Even food is often times, presented as something sexy and alluring. It should hardly be surprising that we - teenaged girls, are emulating what we see in the larger culture.

Talk Back:

Do you like the way you dress?

_____

_____

If yes, what do you like about the way you dress?

_____

_____

If no, what would you like to change?

_____

_____

Do your clothes make you feel empowered (strong, in charge, secure) by today's standard? Why or Why not?

_____

_____

Mom: Try these activities with your daughter:
- Go through the clothing in your closet, see what no longer fits or is out of fashion?
- Model some outfits for her, ask her to give an honest opinion about how you look?
- Do the same for her.
- Determine an appropriate means to discard old clothing: offer them to a family friend or relative with small children, donate to good will, and try consignment.

"It's better to look ahead and prepare than to look back and regret."

Jackie Joyner Kersey, Olympic Champion

CHAPTER 3
EXERCISE & PHYSICAL FITNESS

Tynetta Muhammad

To feel your best exercise is the key. Walking, Jogging, Tennis, Volleyball, Badminton, Swimming, are all great exercises and can be a lot of fun with other people. Spend at least 30 minutes 5 days a week completing some form of exercise.

The USDA recommends at least **60 minutes** of physical activity every day. In addition to strength training exercises, they recommend cardiovascular activities like bike riding, walking, swimming, and sports.

Please realize that with today's gaming systems, the television, and of course the internet, teens lack opportunities for exercise. As a teenager, you go through many changes. For one thing, your body is on its way to becoming its adult size. Have you noticed that you cannot fit into your old shoes or that your pants are now 3 inches too short? Along with these changes, you are probably becoming more independent and making more of your own choices. One of the biggest choices you face involves your health.

So why exercise?

Why? Because healthy habits, including eating nutritiously and being physically active, can help you feel good, look good and do your best in school, work or sports. They might also prevent diabetes, high blood pressure, heart disease, osteoporosis, stroke and some cancers when you are older.

What can I do now to keep myself healthy?
- Get regular exercise.
- Eat a healthy diet.
- Always use your seat belt.

- Do not drink and drive. Do not get into a car with a driver who has been drinking alcohol or using drugs.
- Wear protective headgear, such as motorcycle or bike helmets, when participating in sports.
- Talk to your parents or your doctor if you are feeling sad or if you are thinking about harming yourself.
- Avoid situations where violence or fighting may cause you to be physically injured.
- Prolong (delay) having sex. This can prevent many health (not to mention emotional and spiritual) problems with your body. Ask your parent(s) to tell you about sex, their personal experiences and/or perspectives. If they are not comfortable, talk to an adult you trust (an aunt, older sibling, cousin, grandparent or school counselor). You need to know what you may be about to get involved in. Remember the "safest" sex is no sex.
- See a doctor regularly and as necessary.
- Do not use tobacco product or drugs of any kind.

Even just a stroll around the park for an hour can help you in the end. Here are some exercises for you to use whether by yourself or with a friend:

- Walking with friends, walking pets, race or power walking, climbing stairs, walking on treadmills, mall walking, walking while chatting on the phone, walking for special causes like Relay for Life.
- Playing games on the Wii – Wii Fit Plus has games for strength training, aerobics, yoga, and balance, Wii Sports.
- Swimming or water activities like water aerobics, water-skiing, kayaking, surfing, or wake boarding.
- Martial arts like Jujitsu, Tae Bo, kick boxing, yoga, or Tai Chi.
- Playing ball, Frisbee, tag games, relay games, croquet, badminton, or yard darts.
- Roller skating, in-line skating, ice-skating, or cross-country skiing.

However, remember exercising is most effective when you have a good diet. So regardless of how much training you do, you will never reach your full potential if you do not eat right. Do not get trapped in the same fad diet rut that so many adults do. Instead, use your teenage years as a time to establish a lifelong healthy eating lifestyle. Do not starve yourself; however, learn about the benefits of fasting (abstaining from food for short periods of time). Your body needs nourishment to grow properly and to keep your metabolism running. You can even make an exercise and diet log!

Stay away from fast food and other processed foods. They are cheap for a reason. Fill your diet with low fat foods and fresh, leafy vegetables. A good rule to go by is the color on your plate. The more variety of bright colors your plate contains, the more healthy your meal, plus make sure you drink lots of water!

But I can't get sick....right?
Car accidents, unintentional physical injury, homicide and suicide are the top killers of teenagers and young adults. Cancer and heart disease can also affect you at this age. Unplanned pregnancy and sexually transmitted diseases (including HIV and AIDS) can cause you social and personal problems, in addition to harming your health.

A Mom's Vision of Health & Wellness for Her Daughter
Nisa I. Muhammad

The women in my family on my mother's side tend to be chubby. They are figure models on my dad's side. My mother had a weight problem when she was young and if I didn't watch what I ate, it would certainly be a problem for me too. Understanding this, I didn't want my daughter, Majidah, to suffer with weight issues. She may have 99 problems but weight wasn't going to be one of them. I'm a mother of five and while my girls were young I was very careful about what they ate and where they ate it. For optimal health is not only critical to prevention but it is critical to a girl's self –esteem and confidence.

All was going fine with this until my oldest son, Haki, came home one day and said "Majidah ate something off the ice cream truck." "She did what," I asked. "I'm not sure what it was but it was something out of a jar on the ice cream truck," Haki said.

So most ice cream trucks I have ever seen had those sausages in some kind of liquid in the jars just enticing children to buy them. I was grossed by the thought. Many of these products are fatty, full of chemicals, high in sodium and are linked to obesity and cancer. (fooducate.com) So I tell Haki to ask Majidah who was around nine or ten at the time to come inside.

"Majidah, what did you eat off the ice cream truck?," I ask. She gets this deer in the headlights look and responds, "I'm not sure." "You ate something and you don't know what it was." She looks even more scared. This could have been an Incredible Hulk moment for a mom. However, I'm not the kind of mom that screams, yells and hollers. Never wanted to be that kind of mother. I have absolutely no recollection of my mom yelling, screaming, hollering or even cursing at me. That was my example. All she had to do was say it once maybe twice. Never three times or just give us a look.

"I don't think what you ate was appropriate so since you can't determine what meats are appropriate and which ones are not you will not be eating meat again until you are able to distinguish foods to eat and not to eat. You will be a vegetarian and only eat fish. Is that clear?" "Yes ma'am," she answered.

That is how Majidah (and our family) became a vegetarian and to this day at 27 even though she can distinguish foods, she is still a vegetarian. I use this story as a lead in to my advice for moms.

First, I advise moms to make your home party central. So I would not have to worry about young children eating this or that at their friend's homes, our home was the place to be. Invite all of your friends, whatever the occasion; let's do it at our house. This worked out very well for me because not only could I control the menu I could also control the behavior and activities. Children have social lives, which are fine, but for me it was better to be involved and manage their social activities so I could also manage their consumption.

Moms cannot leave any aspect of their daughter's life to happenstance. I had and still do have a vision for my daughter. I know what kind of girl I wanted her to be and what kind of young woman I want her to be. She has exceeded all of my expectations and prayers. I thank God for having a bigger vision for me than I could ever have. But it all started with my vision for her coupled with me creating the experiences to help her get there.

Back to health and fitness. So as she was growing, now as a vegetarian, I saw that she was gaining some weight. How do you gain weight as a vegetarian? Go figure. Too many sweets, not enough physical activity/exercise, I suppose. As I mentioned, women on my mother's side have weight issues and I was concerned that my daughter may have inherited those genes. I decided to not take chances.

So second, I advise moms, to enroll your daughter in a physical activity. Here's how my conversation with my daughter went:

MOM: "Majidah, I signed you up for a soccer team."

DAUGHTER: "I don't know how to play soccer."

MOM: "That's ok, they will teach you and you will spend lots of time running up and down the fields."

So Majidah spent a season playing soccer and lost her baby weight. She won an award for most improved player. She came in the game using her hands and left the game using only her feet. She was also more confident and full of laughter.

MOM: "You did really good sweetie. I'm so proud of you."

I decided that if she continued to gain weight that I would find other physical activities to put her in."

Finally, as the mother you must take charge of every area of your child's development and life. Take charge of your post as a mother and create the wonderful and amazing adults God has destined them to be.

Help her grow and develop into the person you want her to be. Remember, children only know what children know and that is why God entrusts them to parents who are supposed to know better. Once they are grown they have the rest of their lives to do whatever they want to do. Give your children a good foundation. Mine did everything I wanted them to do whether they liked it or not. In the end most times they liked it. I was not worried about pleasing my children even though I wanted them to be happy. I was concerned about them having a variety of life experiences that would shape them to be productive citizens for our nation. I was not trying to create a headache for some other mothers' son, daughter, or our community.

A Daughter's Call & Response to being Physically Fit and Healthy
Majidah Muhammad

"Suck in your tummy!" "You're getting chubby." "Don't get fat now!" Growing up in a community full of my aunties and women who love me, I heard from them very often these words. At the time, the constant nagging annoyed me. But looking back, I know it was out of love and concern for my health. The women on both sides of my family tend to hold weight in their stomach and have fuller figures. Due to these genes, my mom was always concerned about my weight and wanted to make sure I was not gaining too much weight.

When I was in fifth grade, my mom noticed that I put on some weight. She immediately signed me up for soccer.

MOM: "I signed you up for soccer. You have to get this weight off. You'll be doing lots of running up and down the field."

DAUGHTER: "What!? Soccer!? I don't even know how to play."

Initially, I was not thrilled about having to play a sport I was unfamiliar with. By the time I got to my first practice, I was overjoyed about the experience. My mom bought me the entire uniform I needed to perform. I remember even yelling at my brother to "get off my shin guards!!" I was not the best player out there, but I was definitely the MOST IMPROVED. When the season ended, I was playing with my feet and not my hands.

Majidah's first rule for daughters, mommy knows best.
God has chosen for us parents whom He has entrusted to love and care for us. Our mothers in particular, are our

first teachers and are meant to guide us in the right direction. Most of the time when they are making us do something we don't like or want to do, it is for our benefit. My mother had a vision for me and provided me with an array of experiences to help bring that vision into fruition. Many of the things she made me do, I went kicking and screaming. By the end of the experience, I had a better understanding of why she wanted me to go through it.

In the same year she made play soccer, she also made me become a vegetarian due to my poor choice of foods at the ice cream truck. I was furious with my brother for tattling and more annoyed with my mom (although I still snuck to eat chicken from time to time at school... lol!).

Majidah's second rule for daughter, eat to live!

Becoming a vegetarian was probably the best decision my mom made for me. The Honorable Elijah Muhammad taught us how to eat the live. Removing meat from our diet is one of the ways to live a longer life. Eating healthy meals full of fruits and vegetables provides nutrients to your body. These nutrients give you energy, keeps your heart beating, your brain active, and your muscles working.

Constant external reminders about weight and eating proper foods, has turned into intrinsic motivation for me to remain healthy. I read labels, make things from scratch when I can and exercise at least 3 times a week.

As my mom was telling me about my weight, I wondered if she was looking in the mirror herself. Instead of criticizing her weight influxes, I suggested we workout together. We would wake up early to run in our neighborhood and she even joined a gym.

Majidah's final rule for daughters, stay active WITH your mom.

Moms need help, encouragement, and reminders too. If you already have an active routine, suggest she join you sometimes. Cook a healthy meal for her. Buy her a gym membership for her birthday. Take her to a trampoline park or just walk in the neighborhood with her. Whatever you do, make it fun! Exercise not only controls your weight, it combats health conditions, improves your mood, boosts your energy and is a great way for mothers and daughters to bond.

Talk Back:

Do you think you have a good diet (foods you eat) ? If not, what needs changing?

_____

_____

_____

_____

_____

_____

"Enjoy the age you are; you'll never be that age again!"

Toni S. Muhammad

CHAPTER 4
"ME TIME"

Schedule me time for special baths, pedicure/manicure, mediations, reflective writing, reading a special book or just lounging around in a quite space at home, in the yard or in a park.

Encourage your daughter(s) to mediate, keep a journal. Sit with them in peace and quiet. Conversations are not always necessary or warranted. Just simply enjoy being in each other's presence. Do not force a lot of activities and programs on your daughter. She does not need to be on a schedule all the time. Let her have time to figure out what she likes, wants to do sometimes, and guide her.

Once a girl turns 13, you can take her to activities at the library, book clubs and community programs to enjoy with other girls. This gives her the opportunity to be around other girls in a structured setting with set beginning and ending times.

Time Alone (girl to girl)
Ava Muhammad
It is good to help others but sometimes you need to spend time by yourself.

I love to spend time by myself with no one around to disturb me. I am one of those people who hate to sit around listening to people talk unless what they are saying is of any relevance. Peace and quiet is more of what I enjoy. Even if only for a few minutes a day, you should go in to your room and do a silent activity. That means reading a book, meditating, drawing, or doing one of your own small little hobbies. You could even go farther where you take an entire day out of your week do something fun and it does not have to be alone. Your friends and you could spend that day together doing something you all like to do.

Me Time (girl to girl)

Tynetta Muhammad

Life is full of stressful things. Being young does not make you immune to stress. Whether you are stressed out for a specific reason or are just feeling beaten down in general the coping strategies are pretty much the same. As a teen, you may feel bombarded with parents, peers, and pressure from everyday life but it is essential that you have a time when it is just YOU. This allows you to focus and learn about yourself so you can sort out the problems or stressors of yourself. Too much bad stress can have a negative affect on one's body, mind, and feelings. How you handle your stress has a lot to do with your health. When stress becomes too frustrating and lasts for long periods, it can become harmful distress. Recognizing the early signs of stress, and doing something about, can improve the quality of your life.

SOME SIGNS OF STRESS

Physical (body)	Mental (mind)	Emotional (feelings)
❖ Headaches	❖ Lack of Concentration	❖ Bored
❖ Nervousness	❖ Forgetfulness	❖ Anger outbursts
❖ Rashes		❖ Nightmares
❖ Stomachaches	❖ Drop in school performance	❖ Sad/depressed
❖ Fast heartbeat	❖ Unable to study	❖ Scared
❖ Perspiration	❖ Carelessness	❖ Withdrawn
		❖ Fighting

Me time allows stress whether it good or bad to be understood.

Here are some ways to handle too much stress

- Take deep breaths/Practice deep breathing exercises
- Watch your thoughts/think positive
- Find time to relax and cool out
- Pray or read something inspirational
- Visualize what you want to happen
- Use pressure points to reduce headaches
- Talk problems over with a friend or counselor
- Don't dwell on your weaknesses
- Feel proud of your accomplishments

- Exercise daily
- Do muscle tension relaxation exercises
- Punch a pillow, scream or kick a can
- Prepare for tests early
- Eat a nutritious meal or snack
- Take one thing at a time
- Set realistic goals
- Stop worrying about things that may never happen
- Learn from your mistakes
- Forgive yourself and others
- Get involved with things you like to do
- Make time for fun
- Perform community service, do something for others

Or

- Use the five steps to problem solve:

1. Brainstorm solutions
2. Think of the consequences
3. Choose a solution
4. Apply the solution
5. Evaluate your choice

Talk Back:

What "Me Time" activities can you do to handle the stress in your life?

1._____

2._____

3._____

4._____

5. _____

"Worry is interest paid on trouble before it is due."
Miriam Makeba

"A problem not worth praying about is not worth worrying about."
Azie Taylor Morton

"There is no free lunch. Don't feel entitled to anything you don't sweat and struggle for."
Marian Wright Edelman

CHAPTER 5
TALKING WITH PARENTS

Have a conversation with your parents. Conversation means talking something over and not talking someone out of something.

While you are on the internet read the latest articles about children and their parents. Share that with your parent. Even if they do not listen, they will be impressed that you took the time to learn about their challenges as a parent and your willingness as a child to help them out by becoming a better child.

Do not judge your parents. Just gently remind them that they once were teenagers too. Ask them about their first time being away from home, first crush, and other significant first.

Talking with Parents (girl to girl)
Tynetta Muhammad
Talking to an adult about any problem can be difficult. You may feel like you will not be understood or that they are clueless to the situation that you want to explain. Sometimes, we feel it is even easier to talk to our peers.

The thing is almost everyone goes through a time when they feel no one understands their problems but you can help you parents understand by:

1. Finding a time that you and your parents can be comfortable and relaxed together.
2. Make sure no one is focusing on something else while you are together. No paying bills, playing Playstation, making dinner, or watching TV!
3. These first two steps might take some effort and patience. So be persistent.

4. If you just want to shoot the breeze try to bring up something, they are interested in. Ask them questions about their day and then bring up the topic YOU want to talk about.
5. If you have something specific you want to talk about let, them know exactly what it is. Do not beat around the bush.
6. If they react badly to what you tell them really, listen to them. Do not react back.
7. Let them finish and do not interrupt. Ask them to do the same for you.
8. When you feel like you have told them what you wanted to, thank them for listening. Remain respectful and keep your voice calm even if you are upset.
9. If you feel like there are still things that need to be talked about, set up a time with them to talk about it another day. Do not continue talking if things have grown tense. Calm down and try to have the talk again at another time.

Other Tips:
1. Show them respect by focusing your attention on the conversation, looking them in the eyes, and by not being sarcastic or rolling your eyes.
2. Be honest. Honesty builds trust. In addition, life is good when your parents trust you.
3. Stay cool. If you stay calm when things get heated up you are showing maturity and your parents will respect that.

Parents should try to understand you no matter what and few things can be as frustrating as having your parents not respect you a developing individual. As a teen, you are trying hard to find your own place in the world. Making decisions for yourself, be those choices good or not so good, is something that helps you do that.

Your parents have been teens, they know that you may make mistakes but they want you to learn from them and want to hear all about your frustrations' so that they can help. So talk to your parents and try to understand things from their point of view as much as possible.

Get comfortable talking with your parents

Ava Muhammad

For many girls, it is very hard to communicate with their parents. We as teens sometimes think our parents do not understand us and never will. Yes, they have lived longer than we have but that does not mean they had the same experiences as us. Another common reason for us not communicating with our parents is because we feel intimidated {whether we admit it or not, sometimes we feel inferior to them}. The simple fact is because they are our parents we feel this way sometimes even if they do not try to make us feel this way. Next time, remember these basic ideas when talking to parents:

1. **Look them in the eye during your conversation with your parents!** Even though you might be listening look at your parent in their eye is a good way to let them know you are listening!

2. **Say your opinion in a respectful way.** It is important for you to be able to express yourself to your parents, just make sure you are respectful!

3. **Speak the truth!** Your parents might not always agree with what you have to say but they respect you for being truthful with them.

4. **Listen!** When you have a conversation with someone you have to listen and so do they.

It may be hard for you to communicate at first but many great things are hard to achieve.

Talk Back:

Discuss a time when it was difficult to talk to parents:

_____

_____

_____

What topic(s) or issue(s) you might find difficult to talk with your parents about?

1. _____
2. _____
3. _____
4. _____
5. _____

What topic(s) or issue(s) you might find easy to talk with your parents about?

1. _____
2. _____
3. _____
4. _____
5. _____

"If you always do what you always did, you will always get what you always got."
Jackie "Moms" Mabley

"Believe in yourself, right from the start
You'll have brain
You'll have a heart
You'll have courage
To last your whole life through."
Lena Horne/Diana Ross from The WIZ

"Mere belief counts for nothing unless carried into practice."
Holy Quran

"You can't get out what you don't put in."
Toni S. Muhammad

CHAPTER 6
SELF ESTEEM

Meditation

Read daily affirmations to build your level of confidence. Some of my favorite authors are Dennis Kimbro and Iyanla Vanzant. Daily affirmations can provide you the daily lift and guidance you need and help to focus your outlook on life. I started meditating with my daughters when they were 5 and 6 years old. If they had a disagreement, I would make them sit down, hold hands, and turn on some soft meditative music for at least 5 minutes. They have grown to love meditating as much as I do.

Poise & Demeanor

I recall my first beauty pageant. I really enjoyed the dressing up, the talent portion and the intellect display. Being a beauty pageant contestant can greatly help with poise, posture and confidence. It will also allow you an opportunity to speak before an audience and demonstrate your talents. It teaches you to be conscious of how you smile, talk and walk. Modeling, Balls and other special events can help your daughter gain experiences that shape her self-confidence.

Public Speaking (Presenting yourself before a group)

Public speaking is the process of delivering content to a group of people. It is a reason for getting up in front of people and can inform, persuade and/or entertain. It was nothing for my mom to make us entertain our entire family during family gatherings. My older sister and I (Dr. Toni) sang and my baby sister danced. Therefore, we gained a lot of confidence early in life. We also had fun. I believe my mom was a master of helping her daughters to gain confidence. She would look us directly in the eye when she spoke to us; tell us to pronounce words correctly and to use proper sentence structure. In elementary school, we were in plays, and by the time we reached high school and college, we were in drama, public speaking, talent shows, musicals and band. There were so many opportunities and she encouraged us to participate in every one of them.

Girls, here are some tips to nurture your public speaking confidence:

- ❖ Discover your artistic side. Do you like to sing, draw, paint, play an instrument, dance, and write/recite poetry? If there is a chance to provide entertainment at family gatherings or other events, do it and take advantage of opportunities to display your talent. This is a great confidence builder.
- ❖ Get involved in community and school events that will allow you to display your skill or talent. Be sure to ask your parent's permission.
- ❖ Write down what you want to say, or do before getting up in front of others.
- ❖ Have some pre-scripted ideas for on the spot moments. This requires you to reflect about things that are important to you.

- ❖ Stand in front of a mirror with something to read. Place your hand to your side and read slowly, and with strength.
- ❖ Remember to breathe comfortably so that you can speak clearly.
- ❖ Practice opening and closing your mouth to gain greater control over the voice box.
- ❖ Practice often because a day will come that you have to speak in front of people. No one wants to be a bad public speaker.
- ❖ Every chance you get, show off. Develop a motivational point/inspiration point – something that gets you excited, enthusiastic and charged up.
- ❖ At family gatherings, make it a point to talk to everyone. Keep up with current events, talk about yourself, such as what you're involved in and your plans.
- ❖ Observe (watch) other great speaks, including family members. Take mental notes of body language, voice pitch (loudness) and tone (the attitude when speaking). Visualize (imagine) yourself being as good as they are and even better.
- ❖ Study, read, research. The more you know, the

more you can reference (a knowledge base to draw from and get ideas). The more you put in, the more you get out.

Mom Hints: Pay attention to personality traits displayed by your daughter as much as possible. Notice her, how she acts and responds to others, what activities she seems to take a strong interest in or likes, you can take advantage of those times to guide and nurture her development. Coordinate and conduct family entertainment. Find out if other children/teenagers want to put on a talent show for the family and you are the M.C. Include the children in family events and give them the chance to build their self-esteem as well.

Keeping A Journal

Dr. Jacqueline Dennis

A mother raising a daughter can be extremely challenging, especially opening lines of communication. Communication is the key in having a successful relationship with your daughter. When your daughter reaches her teenage years, which may be viewed as the turbulent teens, mothers must arm themselves with slang, teen speak, and get involved with as many "youth" activities as possible. Mom must practice patience and caution to begin the battle of the pre-teen and teenage wits and not take what she perceives as rebellion or disrespect, personally. These are opportunities to learn, grow and appeal to your daughter's love for you and her desire to be loved.

Beginning at ages 9-12 marks the initiation of the battle of the teenage wits. It is the beginning of an uphill battle with your daughter seeing eye to eye on what, when, how and why turbulent teens should start opening lines of communication to begin to understand respect, obedience and compromise for a relationship with their mother.

To work towards closing the gap on the aforementioned, a mother could give her daughter a diary as a gift and monitor her use of it discreetly in a positive way.

*The diary should **not be used** as a tool for control **only** concern.*

The mother and daughter could sit together occasionally and discuss some of her daughter's entries in the diary reassuring her daughter that the discussion will not result in a backlash, criticism, stereotype or labeling her in a negative light. The discussion should be filled with open discussion, knowledge and education. This positive activity could lead to an honest and respectable relationship between the two of you.

Keeping a Journal (girl to girl)
Tynetta Muhammad

Keeping a journal is one of the best things you can do in regards to reflecting on your life. A journal can help you better understand yourself as a person. When you think of journals, you think of a girl writing about how her day was, whom she interacted with and what she did. However, a journal is much more than that; it can be used to keep a daily log of what you eat so you make healthier choices.

Although it may be difficult to write every day in your journal, it is important that you write in it as much as possible. Why? Because you want your memories to be as fresh as possible when writing. A journal also enables you to recount important dates and events in case you need to. A journal will allow you to get it all out and all down. The act of purging through the writing process (be it with a pen or a keyboard) offers a type of cleansing that discussion may not seem to solve.

Types of Journals

1. Notebook and Bound Books
The most common way of recording journal entries is by hand in a notebook. You can buy a nice notebook or just use a simple one such as a spiral bound or three ringed binder. I have used all types and prefer ones where I can fold the left flap around to the back, making the folder smaller and easier to write on. Bound books are great too because they sturdier and usually last longer.

2. Computers/Blogs
Typing your journal entries can be a quick and easy way to record your life history. Any word processing program works great, even the basic "notepad" in Windows would make a great journal. Be aware that you will have to back up your work often and eventually print it to keep it safe. Printed entries can be easily put into three ring binders, or if you like to write many entries you could place them in a labeled box.

3. Letters and Emails
Do you write a lot of emails or letters? If so then make sure you keep a copy for your journals! Print your emails or copy letters before you send them and place them into a folder or binder. Sometimes I write long, detailed letters/emails that I paste a copy of right into my journal, which saves me from having to rewrite everything. If you are sending lots of letters home (as missionaries do) make, sure your family keeps them so you can add them to your journal.

4. Scrapbooking
Do you love taking many photographs? Scrapbooking is a wonderful (and popular) way to record your life. Working with your pictures is fun and creative, but if you do not journal you will miss all the important details. While scrapbooking just ask yourself these questions, "If someone saw this page 50 years from now would they know who these people/places are? Would they know how I felt?" If the answer is no then you need to add journaling to your scrapbook page.

5. Media Sources
Journal recording can be lots of fun when you use other media sources such as tape recorders, video tapes, and digital video clips on the computer. The biggest concern is to make sure you protect your data. If you do lots of this type of journaling, make sure you keep everything labeled and organized. Keeping an index of descriptions for each recording would help keep the journaling alive.

6. Spiritual or Gratitude Journal
Keeping a Gratitude Journal is a great way to show thanks to God. What you do is record the spiritual events in your life (or that of your family and friends) along with your personal thoughts and ponderings. Write down your experiences, answers to prayers, your testimony, conversion, and other spiritual experiences from church/temple attendance and scripture study.

When you journal daily of your blessings and what you are thankful for you will be amazed at your spiritual growth.

7. Study Journal
Elder Richard G. Scott said, "Knowledge carefully recorded is knowledge available in time of need. Spiritually sensitive information should be kept in a sacred place that communicates to the Lord how you treasure it. This practice enhances the likelihood of your receiving further light."

8. Meeting Journal
I like to carry around a small notebook for keeping notes during church meetings. This helps me focus on the talks and lessons at church, and gives me a place to record my thoughts and reflections as they happen.

9. Calendars
Calendars can be great additions to your journal. You can use the kind that come with planners, ones that hang on the wall, or even the kind that fit in a purse or backpack. Calendar entries have to be short to fit in the space, but work great for keeping track of important events in life. Just make sure you keep your calendars when the year's over and place them with your journals.

10. Additional Embellishments
Journal writing can be fun when you decorate your journal/pages, attach important documents, and even make your own maps when describing a detailed location. If you like statistics, make your own charts and graphs to keep in your journal.

Source: Retrieved on August 2010 from
http://lds.about.com/od/1/a/les_journal.htm

Talk Back:

Journal questions to ask yourself:

1. What happened today that made me sad/mad/happy?
_____
_____

2. What do I like the most about myself?
_____
_____

3. What do I like to do in my free time?
_____
_____

4. What type of exercises did I do today?
_____
_____

5. What do I like about home?
_____
_____

6. What don't I like about home?
_____
_____

7. Why is my best friend my best friend?

_____

_____

8. What did I eat today?

_____

_____

9. Was it nutritious?

_____

_____

10. What talents do I have?

_____

_____

Remember, a journal is kind of like a mirror that reflects an image of our inside instead of our outside. We cannot really look inside ourselves unless we have our thoughts, habits, personality, beliefs, and other things that make up our person on paper. We can learn a great deal about ourselves by reading our own journals. So start yours today!

> **"If you want to be a millionaire, you have to think like one."**
> *Dr. Johnnie Coleman*

> **"Life doesn't have to be a struggle."**
> *Marian Anderson*

> **"Stretch your hands as far as they reach, grab all you can grab."**
> *Yoruba Proverb*

> **"Luck is what happens when preparation meets opportunity."**
> *Unknown*

> **"Ask and it shall be given you…"**
> *Matthew 7:7*

CHAPTER 7
FINANCES & MONEY

A girl needs her own money. She should be encouraged to begin thinking about ways to use her skills and talents to earn her way. Allowances are a good start; however, with all of the demands girls can place on their mothers, its time to come up with creative ways for girls. Here are a few:

- Arts and crafts
- Sewing/clothes making
- Jewelry making
- Photographer

- Videographer
- Website development/maintenance
- Blog development/maintenance
- Snack shop/stand
- Raffle tickets
- Babysitting
- Host a Mom's night out at a community center or your home.
- Other nationalized fundraisers

Girls can make money in ways that their parents may be unable to. For example, mothers may want to start a small home based business and pay their daughter(s) for providing service or working a couple of hours to check email, draft letters, create flyers and even update their website.

Money and Finances
Ava Muhammad
We all want our own money but are to young to work so what do you do? They have many ways for teens to earn money even if you do not acknowledge it.
Here is a list of ways you can earn money:

1. Start an eBay business sell some of that old junk cluttering up your room.

2. Babysit {make sure you inform your parents before taking a job}.

3. Sell hand made jewelry.

4. Photograph and videotape people events for a small price.

5. Snack shop/stand.

6. Website development/maintenance.

7. Blog development/maintenance.

8. Learn how to style hair.

9. Have a neighborhood snack stand

10. Tutor in subjects that you earn high marks in.

11. Be a photographer for family and friends for a small fee.

12. Do face painting and sketching.

Talk Back:

Journal questions to ask yourself:

1. What talents and/or skills do you have?

_____

_____

_____

_____

2. Have you ever used these talents and/or skills to earn money? If yes, describe. If no, what would it take for you to get started?

People:_____

Tools/Equipment:_____

_____

Other Resources:

_____

_____

_____

3. What type of career/occupation do you see yourself working? And, why?

_____
_____

_____
_____

"They try to make me hate myself because I am different but that makes me love me even more!"
Ava M. Muhammad

"When self respect takes its rightful place in the psyche, you will not allow yourself to be manipulated by anyone."
Indira Mahindra

"People may doubt what you say, but they will always believe what you do."
Nannie Helen

CHAPTER 8
FRIENDS & ASSOCIATES

Social Networking

Social networking is the coolest thing since sliced bread and not many of us can remember when bread was not sliced! Well, let me tell you why you want to social network. It is free, it is fun and it is a great network opportunity. You can meet people from all over the world who share similar interest, career aspirations and goals. It can lead to business opportunities. Quick tips to remember:

- ❖ Be respectful toward yourself and others. Avoid using profanity and derogatory language.

- ❖ Restrict access of certain information such as when your home, when your parents are away, etc.

- ❖ Do not friend all your co-workers, schoolmates and everyone that send you a friend request.

The Dangers of Social Networking

Ava Muhammad

Chatting with your friends on these social networking sites may be fun but be careful. As I have pointed out in the section *Friends & Associates* not everybody is your friend. So remember these rules:

1. Never chat with people that you do not know {and parents do not know about and/or approve of}.

2. Never give out any of your personal family information such as family location, parent occupations and schedules, etc.

3. Never answer anything from people you do not know {a girl answered something from some anonymous person and he downloaded all her files on her computer he could also you use the web cam on her laptop to spy on her}.

Please Be Very Careful On Social Networking Sites!

Bullies

Ava Muhammad

100% percent of teens are bullied. The problem is that even if we are a bully, we may have been tormented before in the past. If only people could understand that, everyone is different and no one is the same. I personally think we could all get along but that is not the only problem. The stereotypes of being skinny or fat, light skinned or dark skinned, how you style your hair and clothing are just a few things that create opportunities for bullying. Then there is the problem that the people who are bullied, never speak up about it and the bullies who torment other people usually have very low self- esteem/self-esteem issues.

Be forewarned that in some states, bullying is a crime. (Visit http://www.stopbullying.gov/laws/ for more information.) However, if someone bullies you, immediately talk to an adult or a mentor about how to handle it.

Talk Back:

Journal questions to ask yourself:

1. What is my goal when I represent my self to people?

_____

_____

_____

_____

2. What impression might others have about me based on my social network pages? And, why?

Great   Good   Okay   Needs Improvement

_____

_____

Tynetta & Ava

"As a man (girl) thinketh in her heart, so is she."
Proverbs 23:7

"Each one, reach one, teach one."
African American Proverb

"You're not obligated to win. You're obligated to keep trying to do the best you can every day."
Marian Wright Edelman

"Each day is God's gift to you. What you do with it is your gift to Him."
T.D. Jakes

CHAPTER 9
SCHOOL

School (Girl to Girl)

Tynetta Muhammad

The truth is that many children do not like school except for the element of interaction (hanging around friends, etc.) but the entire nation is painfully aware that a growing number of students experiencing school failure are African American. Statistics indicate that every seven seconds of the school day an African-American student is suspended from public school. Every forty-nine seconds of the school day, an African-American student drops out of school.

Many of us know that education is important because it can open doors for you but education also enlightens and empowers, gives new perspectives, and gives us knowledge of the outside world and our history! With education, our opinions can have justification and backing. Education informs us that everything has a discipline and is a skill. Nevertheless, education is not just going to school; it is a life long journey that you go through everyday. Many do not know but the word education is derived from *educare* (Latin) "bring up", which is related to *educere* "bring out", "bring forth what is within", "bring out potential" and *ducere*, "to lead" so your education should bring you to your fullest ability and bring out the brilliance that is within you.

Do you like school? If yes why? If no why not?

_____
_____
_____
_____

There are many types of learning styles some include:

- **Visual (spatial).** You prefer using pictures, images, and spatial understanding.
- **Aural (auditory-musical).** You prefer using sound and music.
- **Verbal (linguistic).** You prefer using words, both in speech and writing.
- **Physical (kinesthetic).** You prefer using your body, hands and sense of touch.
- **Logical (mathematical).** You prefer using logic, reasoning and systems.
- **Social (interpersonal)**. You prefer to learn in groups or with other people.
- **Solitary (intrapersonal).** You prefer to work alone and use self-study.

(http://www.learning-styles-online.com/overview/)

Find yours because it is good to know so that you are learning to your fullest potential! Moreover, it is okay to have more than one.

My learning style is/are_____

_____
_____
_____

Career Options

Ava Muhammad

School can help us pick a certain career to go in to but school is not what motivates all of us. The thing is that we do not take life or our education seriously enough. When you ask most girls what they want to be I often hear them say a singer. That is fine but don't you think we have enough entertainers. Why not an engineer or a doctor, both helps others in their professions. When I have suggested that to other girls, they say they want to be famous. Well you could cure some big disease that would make you famous or why not invent something. You do not have to be a singer or actor to be great. As we get older what we want to be when we grow up changes. One day we want to be a doctor the next day we want to be a hair stylist, our opinions may keep changing but remember, the only limits we have come from ourselves.

School can help you grow socially into the person you are to become in your life. Who you hang out with can influence you in your adolescences and young adulthood as well as determine several of the life paths or career paths you might take. In the end, you must find what you are passionate about and surround yourself with positive people who will help you get to where you want to be in your life. As you enter into high school, you should pick specific courses that will help you further your knowledge about the career you want. However do not be afraid to explore new things and options because you might find that you like to do something else more.

Tynetta - High School Graduate Class of 2014

"Whatever we believe about ourselves and our ability comes true for us."
Susan L. Taylor

"Successful people succeed because they learn from their failures."
Bettina Flores

"Just don't give up what you're trying to do. Where there is love and inspiration, I don't think you can go wrong."
Ella Fitzgerald

CHAPTER 10
AROUND THE HOUSE LIFE SKILLS

Cooking

Tynetta Muhammad

Cooking is a fun activity that everyone should experience because everyone likes to eat. In today's time with fast food and pre-made dinners, it is easy to see why so many people cannot and will not cook or see cooking as a chore. However, cooking your own food is important and it is a skill that you should learn while you are young.

Besides, when you cook you always know what goes into your food and it is so much healthier. Before you start, first you must find the time to cook and have all your ingredients ready. If you can, it is best to use fresh ingredients! It will excite you watching the butter melt in your pan/skillet, just do not let it burn you. Cooking is not difficult and you will love to watch as your food that you are making bakes, broils, fries, and boils in its pot, skillet, or pan. You can even make your own recipes using your favorite types of food instead of following someone else's.

Many know you can cook meats and vegetables but did you know you could cook fruit not only by baking but also by stir-frying them. Sometimes you can even amaze your parents by serving them dinner. You should make it a family thing and get your parents involved in helping you cook or at least let them supervise.

Fun foods to begin with:

- Macaroni & Cheese
- Spaghetti & meat sauce (meat balls)
- Muffins (blueberry, banana, farina)
- Onion Rings or French fries
- French Toast and Eggs
- Mashed Potatoes
- Creamy Corn

Cleaning

My mother always tells me that cleanliness is close to Godliness. What does that mean? It means that our creator has designed and provided us with the most effective and productive natural environment wherein there is cleanliness (order and organization that leads to a fresh, sparkling, uncontaminated, pure, spotless environment) and not un-cleanliness (disorganization, confusion, chaos, dirty, soiled, and contaminated). When we observe nature, we find the evidence of how God has organized and arranged everything beautifully and in harmony for us to enjoy – meaning that when we interact with our environment it is most pleasing to all of our senses – seeing, hearing, smelling, tasting and touching.

Although many teens may not fully understand all the ins and outs of cleanliness, it is very important to learn how to keep a clean room and a clean house. A clean house will also keep allergens from accumulating, boost your mood and help you understand the value of the things that you own. Additionally, there is nothing like having a guest to visit you and find that your room and home reflect a high level of care and harmony. When guest come to visit you, you will feel less self conscious because your house is clean and everything is in order versus if your house is dirty and chaotic (out of order).

Cleaning is as simple or as complicated as the area. It can go from wiping a single area down with a disinfectant wipe or clean towel to using more aggressive cleaning solvents (always read the instructions) and polishing furniture or floors until they shine. Always remember to be careful when handling chemical cleaning supplies as these supplies can be detrimental to ones health.
Breathing in bleach, ammonia, or glass cleaner or getting it in the eyes can permanently damage the lungs or blind you. Never over-exert yourself when cleaning around

chemicals and always keeps doors or windows open, especially when cleaning in a confined space such as a bathroom.

Keeping a clean house and room will let your parents know that you are responsible and care for the things that are in your possession.

Talk Back:

Journal questions to ask yourself:

1. What do I cook well right now?

_____

_____

2. What do I want to learn to cook?

_____

_____

3. Have you ever considered using cooking talents and/or skills to earn money? If yes, describe. If no, what would it take for you to get started?

People:_____

Tools/Equipment:_____

_____

Other Resources:

_____

_____

_____

4. Rate how clean your room is?
Excellent   Good   Needs Improvement   Poor

5. How important is a clean house or room to you?
Extremely   Somewhat   Needs Improvement   Not Important At All

Explain your answer:
_____
_____

_____
_____

6. Rate how clean your house is?
Excellent   Good   Needs Improvement   Poor

7. Is the kitchen sink free of dishes and counter tops clean?

Yes   Somewhat   No

8. Are things/objects in the floor? Yes   No   Somewhat

Yes   Somewhat   No

9. Is there dust/dirt buildup on surfaces?

Yes   Somewhat   No

10. Are books on shelves, whatnot's in there places?

Yes   Somewhat   No

11. Are clothes put in drawers/ hung up in closets?

Yes   Somewhat   No

12. Are shoes put in closet or other designated place/

Yes   Somewhat   No

13. Please describe the general condition of your house. And, what you can do to improve it?

_____
_____

_____
_____

_____
_____

_____
_____

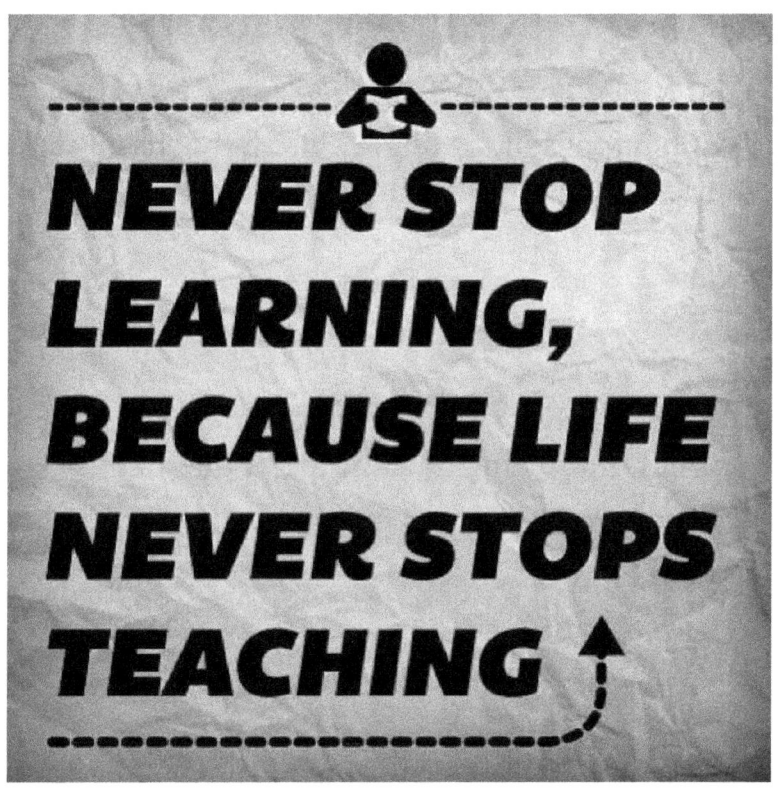

"Defining myself, as opposed to being defined by others, is one of the most difficult challenges I face."
Carol Moseley-Braun

"Diversity is not about how we differ. Diversity is about embracing one another's uniqueness."
Ola Joseph

"Trust yourself. Think for yourself. Act for yourself. Speak for yourself. Be yourself. Imitation is suicide."
Marva Collins

50 TIPS FOR MOTHERS AND DAUGHTERS

Tynetta 17, Dr. Toni & Ava 16

Each of these tips come from personal experiences growing up, rearing my two daughters, observing others rearing their daughters and knowledge that I have acquired from my personal and professional studies.

I have tried every one of them, some I have implemented more successfully than others. ☺ However, I believe and know that others can benefit from this information, perhaps improve upon it for greater success in rearing their daughters.

Mothers

1. **Pay attention to what your daughter says, what she does and how she does it!** If she does not do it, the way you want her to do "it" then you must show her the correct way. It is easy to criticize but better to demonstrate. Learn the importance of being objective and neutral so she will be more receptive to your guidance. Offer constructive feedback not criticism.

2. **Tell your daughter how beautiful she is every day! Help her gain confidence in herself, her looks, early.** When she looks at you, she is looking in the mirror. Reflect back to her the confidence she needs to build her self-esteem. Tell her she is beautiful and that she is special to God's plan.

3. **Be your daughters' parent, first, if you want to build a real and genuine friendship!** A girl needs nurturance and guidance from you that reflects your confidence and poise as a mother. She must know that you have the skills and courage about rearing her to become a successful young lady and adult. Then, she can trust you to be their friend.

4. **Encourage your daughter to express herself!** Teach her to be assertive and unafraid to display the best of herself around others. Let her know

how her unique perspective is highly valued. She wants to know that you value her, as a separate being that one day will have to go for herself. If you start now and let her know that she will have to be independent of you, make certain decisions one day for herself, she can begin to think more critically about her actions and embrace her inner voice and power.

5. Demand that your daughter stand up for herself and the truth! She should be encouraged to speak the truth regardless of who or what. She must also be shown the correct manner and attitude by which to deliver "the truth." Therefore, as a rule tell her to think at least 5 times before she speaks. You want her to develop a bold and brave spirit that resonates her love of honesty and recognizes the critical dynamics of tact.

6. **Demonstrate the character you want your daughter to emulate in private and in public!** Remember it's what you say and what you do that makes the impression on her.

7. **Spoil your daughter with experiences (not things) that encourage her to grow and develop!** Have a spa day at home, enjoy out door time playing volleyball, badminton, tennis, and go to the pool. Pack a lunch and eat at the park. Spend time talking, laughing, getting to know them and letting them get to know you.

8. **Provide your daughter with practical explanations for "why she received this instead of that."** She needs to understand that process is a part of everything and that nothing comes out of a vacuum. So, if you don't let her stay the night with her new school mate, she needs to be

informed that the family rule is that mom (or dad) must know the family of her school mate well enough so that she will be safe from any potential harm. Also, tell her that you would like to meet her schoolmate's parent(s), perhaps meet at a park to get to know each other or join you for an evening movie in the park.

9. **Tell her to enjoy being a girl for as long as she is a girl and let her!** Tell her that each year is special while she is a girl and that she should cherish them. There is no rush for her to be "grown" or act "grown." It is good for her to enjoy this phase of her development for as long as she can because once she reaches an age of maturity and transitions to becoming a young lady, young adult, a wife and/or a mother she will have great responsibility.

10. **Always be honest when she ask your opinion! Be honest, not brutal.** Gently tell her your perspective and always remind her that what she thinks is always just as important.

11. **Expose your daughter to women of different backgrounds and experiences.** Diversity is the key to helping your daughter find personality balance. She needs to witness women who are at different stages of life, a teen girl, a young college age girl, a young adult female, a newly wed female, a married female, a mother with small children, an adult professional woman. All these stages along with their corresponding roles – student, athlete, community volunteer, squad leader, artist (sings, dances, paints) homemaker, coach, teacher/professor, other occupations – helps her know that she has choices about the kind of person she wants to become.

12. **Take your daughter out for fine dining. Let her first experiences be with you not someone else.** By fine dining, we mean a nice sit down restaurant with a server. A buffet does not count toward this experience. Preferably, some place where you receive a cloth napkin, so this gives you many restaurant options. Show her to order, interact with the server by being polite, saying thank you, smiling and the art of tipping. Show her how to have conversation with you by speaking in a tone wherein only you and she know what is being said. Show her that she should visit the restroom to tidy up/freshen up after her meal. Show her how to correctly exit the restaurant by settling the bill and leaving the area without excessive soiled items on the table.

13. **Treat your daughter according to her unique personality and value to your family.** Every girl wants to feel unique and rightly so, because every girl is unique. Each one has her own special reason/purpose for being and each one has to be given individual opportunities to develop her gifts. If you only have one daughter, then observe the daughters of others (your sisters, brothers, friends, associates). Note how girls respond to "things" differently. Some may require a soft touch while some can handle assertive guidance. Some may express interest in many things; others may have only one interest. Some will be social butterflies; others are more observant and less vocal. Some may want to cook for the party; others may want to entertain for the party. Some will be powerhouses of multiple and different combinations. Nonetheless, it is your duty as the

parent to pay attention to these characteristics and guide your daughter(s), even assist other parents, with appropriate opportunities for their development.

14. **Do not compare your daughter to anyone else's daughter or too their sibling(s).** This is a big no, no! As stated in point 13, each girl is unique. Find out by observing what stimulates her, motivates her, how she reacts and responds to different situations. She has her own aptitudes and characteristics to display. She should be encouraged to always discover and find her "truest" self.

15. **Hug, kiss and show affection to your daughter. She needs to feel the warmth of your physical presence.** This will minimize her need to seek affection elsewhere. Some parents may

have not experienced this as children and may find giving affection to their children challenging. Understandable. So do not force it. Just take advantage of the "big" opportunities to show affection like at an award ceremony, graduation, birthday parties, and holidays. There are plenty of these "big" opportunities so take advantage of them. As for the "little" opportunities, well really these are more critical to your daughter's development than the "big" ones. Why? Because, these are the private moments, the ones where she will really feel that you like her as a person, not just love her because she is your child. She needs to know that it is not just a show that you put on in public or in front of company.

16. **Spend special alone time with your daughter. Take her to lunch or tea time away from home.** Visit a coffee or teahouse, a bookstore or invite

her to sit in your room and watch a movie. One on one for her birthday is cool.

17. **Get to know your daughter's closest or best friend (BFF).** And other comrades too. Invite them over, and visit their homes with their parent(s) present. Get to know the friends family as much as you can too.

18. **Respect your daughter's right to privacy.** Just because you can go through your daughters things, does not mean that you should. However, if you have reason to believe you must, be mindful that you may find things (notes, pictures) you do not like. If you do, do not blow up. Calmly talk to her as if she is someone's daughter about your concern. This may help you to remain calm. Think about what you should say to her before you to talk with her. Do not over react or

exaggerate the situation.

19. **Recognize your daughter's accomplishments in front of family and friends.** Celebrate her progress. Relieve her of her shyness by letting her know that it's great when someone can toot her horn.

20. **Listen to your daughter express her frustrations.** No feedback, just listening. Simply state: I understand. If she asks questions, answer the question with a short answer. Always ask if she understands. If she says no, offer additional explanation. Learn how not to lecture.

21. **Give your daughter objective (non-judgmental) feedback when she talks about others and or situations.** It is best not to take sides, especially when it comes to her siblings,

family members, friends, etc. Just offer her the "other" point of view and explain that everyone sees things in their own way based on their own understanding. Let her know that is okay to agree to disagree and that she should strive to be objective (unbiased) as much as possible.

22. **Help your daughter to know and understand the circumstances surrounding her conception, gestation and birth.** As African American mothers, some of us have experienced challenging situations surrounding our children coming into being. As our daughters grow, it is important that they know some sources of their personality idiosyncrasies. This can aid them with indentifying areas to work on for improvement. Your goal as parent is to aid your daughter through this process. She may not understand that you cried a lot while you were pregnant with

her, or that you drink too much orange juice. Whatever the case was, she needs to be properly informed, over a period of time. You can begin sharing this information when she turns 10. Be willing to be as honest as possible, reserving more sensitive matters for later transitions.

The more a girl can know herself, the circumstances surrounding her conception, her gestation, her birth, her delivery, what her mothers state of mind was, her fathers disposition, etc., then she can tweak the aspects of her self and personality that can have the most influence on who she will become as a woman.

23. **Offer your daughter options for handling difficult situations and difficult people.** Let her know that everyone (even the worst among us) have the right to "be" how we are, but she does not have to respond or succumb to ignorance. Let

her know, that it is her right to excuse herself from people and situations at the first sign of a problem. She can offer a positive outlook to counter the negative. Better still she can be mindful not to place herself around situations bound to bring out the worse in her.

24. **When your daughter makes a mistake, lovingly demand that she corrects it.** Be willing and prepared to show her the proper and correct way. She needs you to give her examples so that she does not make repeated mistakes. She may want help with something but she is afraid to ask. Make yourself available to her so that she can become comfortable with asking for your help.

25. **Always be prepared to offer your daughter alternative solutions but let her decide how to solve/resolve her own "problem."** Your role is to

give her as many options or points of views as possible, not to always solve it for her and/or tell her what to do. For example: She has an argument with a friend or sibling and she come to you. Listen, know that you are only hearing her version, and then offer to share possible ways for her to resolve the issue. Being a **PARENT** means advanced <u>preparation</u> <u>aimed</u> to <u>reveal</u>, <u>empower</u>, <u>nurture</u> and <u>train</u> toward adulthood.

26. **Be willing to put your butt on the line for your daughter, when she is proper and correct.**
Your daughter needs assurances that you can and will protect and defend her against brutal and unwarranted insults and attacks. Our girls do not deserve to be mocked, made fun of, called out their names, or any other demeaning or derogatory behavior. In addition, if she shares a concern with you, determine its legitimacy and

respond accordingly.

27. Question your daughter thoroughly before putting your butt on the line for her.
Nothing can be more frustrating for a parent than to rush to the defense of their child and discover they do not have all the "facts." Ask clear specific questions, listen intently, write it down if you need to, but make sure you have determined the legitimacy of what she tells you before you run off and let everyone have it. There will be times when she does not realize how important little details are. It's your business to be thorough.

28. Teach your daughter that her foresight-looking forward/visualizing is more important and critical to her success in life than hindsight – looking back. Tell her hindsight is not 20/20. For example: Ask her to close her eyes, use her imagination and visualize herself doing a certain things as well as the sequence of events that could follow. Have her to share her example with you. Ask her, to re-envision the situation (her action, reaction, interactions) differently. That's what I call foresight and foresight is 20/20.

29. **Teach your daughter that for every action there is an equal and opposite reaction.** Let her know that it is not okay to hit someone, take someone's things, say whatever comes to her mind, go wherever she wants to and behave the way she feels. Inform her that others (you, her siblings, other family members, her friends) can (and will) do the same thing or worse things too. She should strive to follow the golden rule: *"do unto others as you would have done unto you"* or *"treat others the way you wish to be treated."*

30. **Stress the importance of learning life skills while she is young.** When she turns 10 give her chores (washing dishes, sorting/washing clothes) around the house a few days out of the week. Now if she is under 10, encourage her to pick up toys, hang up clothes, to come watch you in the kitchen or to sort clothes for washing. The point is to have her observe you and provide supervised practice. Help her clean out her room, dresser drawers and closet on a regular basis (at least twice a year). This will also minimize instances mentioned in point #18. Explain to her why cleanliness and organization benefits you, her and your family.

31. **Teach your daughter the value of balance in her gender roles and identity.** She should be encouraged to embrace her assertive side and her passive side. She really has more than two sides,

because the personality adjusts and adapts based on our environment, needs, wants, and the people we encounter. Sometimes she may be laid back, on occasion she may express excitement and interest in something and other times, she may have no interest at all. Whatever, disposition she displays, she should know that being a female, a girl and eventually a woman does not mean being a doormat anymore than displaying hyper aggressive attitudes and tendencies to prove she is strong or "bad." If you have women in your life that display a balance of gender roles and identity this is a great asset. She also needs to see women performing in different roles such as stay at home moms, teachers, professors, nurses, doctors, and business owners. Encourage her to embrace all sides of her developing personality and self.

32. **Tell your daughter that she should always be positive and find the best in situations/circumstances.** It is easy to look for the worst and bad in a situation. Help her to realize that when life gives you lemon, you can make lemonade. Share small examples of disappointments you have dealt with and how you overcame. This is also an underlining factor of forgiveness. Forgiveness is critical to her ability to keep moving forward in life and making consciousness good decisions about her interaction.

33. **Be a leader and trendsetter and encourage your daughter to do the same with her friends.** Let her know she is unique and that there is no one like her on the planet. Her life is her opportunity to grow and shine. Give her opportunities to develop courage early in life.

Teach her the value of being her self and developing her own self-expression, attitude and personality.

34. **Protect your daughter's heart from the whispering of others who do not share your outlook on rearing a successful daughter.** Do not allow people to share negative ideas and outlooks with your daughter about who she is and what she does. Some people may mean well, but it's the little things that can undermine your daughter's growth. For example, my daughter knew when she was 10 years old that she wanted to be a doctor and what steps she wanted to take to fulfill her goal. She shared this with an adult female, who was amazed but also told me that she did not think it was "good" for her to be "thinking" about her future so far in advance. Of course, I respectfully disagreed and shared with her that whatever, my daughter shared with her

of her ideas/plans/goals was not of my doing. However, I had carefully planted the seeds of desire for her to express herself, likes and interest, provided the opportunities for her to explore them, and offered critical feedback to assist her with refining her ideas.

35. **Keep your daughters library filled with books about various subjects and promote reading.** Encyclopedias, dictionary, thesaurus, adventure books, self-help, books about cooking, gardening, spiritual books, philosophy, science and history/herstory. She should not just have a television, a cell phone, the radio and the internet. If possible, do not have any of these items in her bedroom. If she likes certain TV shows, movies, you should strive to watch together. If she listens to music, you should listen to the radio to find out what the children are

listening to – ouch, painful. Minimize her time with electronic devices especially when she is under 15. Set boundaries and time limits. Put a bookshelf in her room. Take her to a bookstore and help her pick out something to read.

36. **Have critical thinking conversation and dialogue with your daughter about current issues and/or topics she has interest in.** Sometimes she will let you know what she finds interesting. Do not take the high and mighty, "why I never" attitude. Remember how you felt as a girl when you wanted to talk to your mom (parent) and how you wished they were more receptive (open minded). Discuss the latest music and movies. Allow her to talk. That is truly the only way you are going to make progress and have "real" conversations with your daughter. It may be uncomfortable, annoying and painful at times but

it is worth it.

37. **Do not "baby" your daughter.** Instead, appreciate each stage of her development and prepare "a rites of passage" for each phase. You want her to develop and mature correctly not be 16 and unable to wash her own clothes or boil an egg. For example, when your daughter turns 10, insist that she has a chore such as washing the dishes.

38. **Do not try to "buy" your daughter.** Spend time with her involved in an activity where she can observe and interact with you (and others). If you buy her things, let it be an acknowledgement of something she has done. Surprise her with a special gift sometimes.

39. **Be her first role model and mentor.** Your

daughter should readily recognize you as the person she is striving to be like, dress like, act like, or to be better than you. Show her how to walk, talk, sit, stand and speak. Teach her important values and demeanor associated with being a princess and a queen.

40. **Always tell your daughter how much you need her and how important she is to you and your family.** It is not enough for her to be your daughter. She needs to know that she is special and that your family would not be the same without her.

41. **Plan special celebrations for your daughter major milestones, 1st day of school, Sweet 16, Graduation, College Acceptance, etc.** Bake her favorite cake. Have balloons ready for her when she gets out of school. I used to also buy her

stuffed animals and place them on her pillow. Show up at school unannounced to have lunch with her – take her food you know she likes. Host a cookout at home or at a park. Invite family and her friends. Take her out to dinner. She will like the fact that you are always thinking about her and ready to celebrate her progress, activities or development.

42. **When she is sad, assure her that this too shall pass and that trouble does not last always.** She needs to know that life has its ups and down. She will experience both. However, she must seek balance in her self so that she can appreciate the highs and lows.

43. **Tell her its okay to cry.** And, that life is like riding a wave, eventually, the water washes to shore. So get back on your board and go out to

catch the next wave.

44. **Make sure that your daughter has a loving/positive relationship with her father.** If her father is absent, present her with men (uncle, older brother, other family associates) that have high moral character, who respect girls and women.

44. **Assure your daughter that she has plenty of time to "fall in love" and "date."** Yes, you should let her know this as early as 10 because in today's schools, children are "dating." It is not cute for her to have a "boyfriend" and you should encourage her to get to know herself and love her self before expecting the attention and affection of others. Tell her that when she is more mature (knows her self, her life purpose and what she wants to do with her life); she will have plenty of

time to enjoy love and dating. Tell her about your first crush or first love. She needs to know that you know where she is coming from and that when things didn't go as expected that you survived those experiences.

45. **Encourage your daughter to develop the right outlook on all of her relationships.** Tell her to never take it personal. People come into your life or are in your life for a reason, a season and a lifetime. When she figures out which one a person is, then she has to learn to allow change to occur.

46. **Help your daughter to understand the importance of setting goals daily, yearly or for certain situations.** She needs to learn about the importance of goal setting. Ask her and assist her with setting small goals. Put these on the

refrigerator or on the wall in her room. Use these as a reminder to promote positive behavior.

47. Teach your daughter to treat people the way she wants to be treated. Teach her to be courteous and respectful. Kindness goes a long way, especially when you interact with the public.

48. Show your daughter how to have standards regarding her dress, demeanor and how she conducts herself. Put her in an etiquette class. Instruct her on the do's and don'ts of how to carry herself. Role-play so that she can learn. Ask her what is most important about her self and her image.

49. Instruct your daughter to make good first impressions because first impressions tend to be the most helpful or hurtful. She should have a good attitude, positive demeanor, clean clothes and shoes, neat fingernails and hygiene in check. She should carry a small purse or back pack with her items inside.

50. **Teach your daughter good manners and courtesy as the prerequisite for earning the respect and admiration of others.** Teach her to say thank you, please and to ask for what she wants. This will carry her a long way and into circles where others will desire her company.

Tynetta, 18 with her BFF, Akilah, 18

Daughters

1. **Get to know your mother so that you can better understand yourself.** Most children mimic (pattern themselves after) their parent(s) and even siblings. Talking, walking, mannerism and attitude can also be traits you picked up from your home environment. So pay close attention because once you realize where you get it from you can determine if it's worth keeping and refining or getting rid of it.

2. **Be patient with your mother, sometimes, she is learning while on the job of being your mother.** Rearing children correctly does not come with a manual. Parents make mistakes and are not always sure about what works, so be understanding, not judgmental.

3. **Remember, your mother used to be a girl too. She wasn't always a mother.** And, she has/had a mother. If you can, talk to her mother, to understand what she was like as a girl and review point #1 as it relates to your mother.

4. **Always ask your mother for advice because chances are she can share insights critical to your development and success.** It's better to know where the potholes are in the road before you travel. Save yourself time and maybe pain by just asking what she thinks. Our mothers have seen the world longer than we have and can offer ways to maneuver in the world when the situation gets rough.

5. **Mothers are rare and precious jewels that must be treasured and valued while they live.** Give/bring her flowers (drawn on a card, picked

from the yard or at the park, or if you can buy them) while she lives.

6. **Be the kind of daughter that you hope to have one day.** Having you as a daughter can be a blessing, an experience your mother can look back on one day with happiness. Or, having you as a daughter can be a nightmare, one that she looks back on with pain and heartache.

7. **Honor your mother (respect and listen to what she ask of you) that your days may be long.** Various scriptures speak about honoring your parents and place special emphasis on a child's relationship to their mother. Remember to listen to your mother when she gives her opinion or insight into a situation. When going out in public you should behave in a respectful manner (speaking in a modest tone, not loud) because not

only do you represent your mother but the principles she is teaching you. This also applies to when you are at home or in private. Also see point #6.

8. **Learn what you like to do around the house so that you can play your part to become a helpful and dutiful daughter.** Especially, when mom works (at home or outside the home) she appreciates help around the house. Certain household chores may seem long and daunting, but find the ones you like to do then do them sufficiently and on a consistent basis. Also make sure that you instruct and guide your younger siblings on certain task or chores around the house.

9. **Express kindness toward your mother for her support and love of you.** If she comes to your

game, to your award program, to another special occasion, tell her thank you. Let her know how much you appreciate her being there for you. Also support your mother in all her endeavors and help her with things she may need to be done. Verbally expressing your gratitude towards your mother is good but offering help may really show her how much you care.

10. **Remember that your mother is only looking out for your best interest, even if her point of view differs from yours.** Mom's can give excellent advice about dealing with tough situations. You may not understand what she means at the time, but later when faced with a situation, you will remember and use it.

11. **When in a "sticky" situation, ask yourself, "how would mom handle this?"** If you have a

chance, watch how your mom interacts with others (her mother, siblings, associates and even strangers). You can learn a lot about adjusting your behavior, demeanor, attitude and actions in different situations.

12. **Take time to think about what your mother tells you!** You do not have to always have a response. Just listen, think it over and then ask her questions or give her your perspective after you have thought it over. If you think it over at least 3 times this will improve your chances of being clear. Even consider writing it down in a journal and reading over your thoughts. Do not jump to conclusions. Give yourself time to examine what, why, how, the outcomes and affects your words can have. She also might give good insight into your problem, everyday life, challenges that you may face or just good advice

for later on in your life. Do not ignore her or tune her out. Listen, just as if you would want her to listen to you.

13. **Tell your mother how you feel about major family changes, especially when it affects you.** But understand the final decision is hers (and/or your father).

14. **Respect your mother's right to privacy.** She had a life before your life started and she will continue to have a life separate from yours in some ways. Your mother has this right just like you do and she wants to be respected. If her door is closed to her room, knock before you go in (wait for her to tell you if you can go in or not) and do not go through her things, take her things or use her things without her permission first.

15. **Know that your mother has a life, desires, interest and goals too.** Understand there are things your mother wants to do with her life. Encourage and support your mother as she pursues the things in her life that she wants. While she is fulfilling her life goals be her biggest fan and cheerleader.

16. **Be happy for your mother when she accomplishes something.** Help her celebrate. Celebrate with your mom and congratulate her for everything she accomplishes. Make her favorite meal or offer to give her a manicure. Whatever you decide to do, make sure she knows that you are genuine about how happy you are for her.

17. **Strive to be the source of joy and laughter in your mother's life.** Make her laugh and be happy to see her.

18. **Strive to give your mother a token of your love whether it is a card, a bead, a what-knot, or a homemade gift.** No special occasion needed just because you love her. Mothers appreciate all things. The work of a mother never ends and you can make the rewards endless with the little things.

19. **Never doubt that your mother loves you. She may not always say it but she does.** She may not always show it, but she does. She has her way of giving affection and it may not fit the mass media hype and projection. It may not look like your friends relationship with her mother. So what. Do not compare your mother to anyone else. She is the one chosen by God to be your mother. Love is not always an "I love you" or a hug and kiss but the work your mother does to provide for you and your family.

20. **Know that discipline is not your mother's idea of trying to hurt you.** Discipline means that she wants the best for you and she wants to ensure that you align yourself properly so that you can receive your blessings.

21. **When your mother spends time with you, take advantage of the time to enjoy her company.** Spending time with your mom is very important because our time on this earth is very short. Do not take for granted that she is here today. Take advantage of spending time doing the things that she enjoys.

22. **Sometimes, mom's have bad days.** Allow her time to unwind, blow off steam and relax.

23. **Learn how to cook and clean.** Offer to prepare dinner or tidy up and give mom a break and time to relax. Learning how to cook and clean is something that will help you throughout life.

24. **Strive to minimize arguments with your siblings because it will create a more peaceful home life.** Mother's want their family (especially children) to get along. Learn to give family members (and siblings) personal space to minimize conflict. And if there is a disagreement, learn to listen more than you speak. Reflect over what was said and offer your perspective later.

25. **Tell your mother how much you love and appreciate her, often.** She can never know enough. A little hug, kiss on the cheek, a small token of appreciation, a flower. Just let her know because tomorrow is not promised to us.

26. **Be proud of your mother and take great joy in introducing her to your friends.**

27. **Be polite and courteous in front of company (guest).** Do not embarrass your mother. Treat her the way you want to be treated.

28. **Strive to do your best in school.** Always keep your mother informed about any problems or concerns you have in your academic work.

29. **Inform your mother when you desire to bring guest home.** Advance notice can save you and your mother discomfort and embarrassment.

30. **Clean up behind yourself.** Demonstrate your awareness and appreciation for your home, space and things by keeping them neat and in order. Chaotic home, chaotic mind, chaotic life.

31. **Be grateful and show appreciation for your home.** Do the chores you are asked to do without constant reminders.

32. **Check with your mother before leaving home.** This gives her peace of mind, shows that you respect her and puts her in the best position to represent your whereabouts in any event.

33. **Tell your mother where you are going, where you are at and who you are with.** This information is important in case of emergency.

34. **Tell your mother about school needs and school events as soon as you know.** Leave her a reminder on the refrigerator or ask her where/how she would like a reminder.

35. **Go to spiritual gatherings, community events, and other outings with your mother.**

36. **Think at least three times about what you want to say before you say it.** You do not want to say something you do not mean or accidently to your mother, her family or others.

37. **Develop independence while also realizing your interdependence on your family.** It's okay to come up with ideas and plans about your activities for your self-development.

38. **Be consistent in your actions and attitude.** The more consistent, the better your mother will consider you reliable and trust worthy.

39. **Do not be disagreeable just for the sake of having your way.** Learn to negotiate with your

mother to settle differences. Always listen to her (hear her out). Your pride or saving face is not at stake, but your ability to disagree without becoming hostile and violent demonstrates your ability to handle intense discussion. After all, if you can learn to navigate these occurrences with mom, you can handle them with anyone.

40. **Give your mother compliments.** Show that you are paying attention and notice how she carries herself. Pay her compliments on her style of dress, hairstyle, a meal she prepared, and for just being your mom!

41. **Develop a relationship with God (a higher spiritual being or consciousness).** Study and participate in activities that encourage the feeling of spiritual awareness, ethics and responsibility. It is critical to help your daughter know that God is

the most powerful force who can intervene in her life to aid her on her journey. She must also realize that our creator works through people to guide and shape into the types of purposeful and purpose filled beings.

42. **Associate with positive peers.** Have friendships with other girls (and boys if possible) that model positive and responsible attitudes, actions, behaviors and demeanors. You will be amazed how much influence "being" around others impacts your thinking and outlook. It can also influence things you do, your preferences/taste and people you associate with. So choose wisely.

43. **Share your knowledge with others. Whether its siblings, peers, school group members, younger children, they can benefit from your**

development. It will also make your mother proud to witness your transformation from child to young lady.

44. **Find things at school that interest you and develop positive skills and hobbies.** More accomplishments for mom to witness your successful transformation.

45. **Read, read, read. Develop an extensive vocabulary and higher critical thinking skills.** This will enable you to make other critical transformations that will show mom how you are getting ready to transition into a mature young lady.

46. **Be a leader.** It is important to know how to and when to follow. Being a leader means knowing and understanding what characteristics

and traits will prepare you for happiness and success and which ones can lead to challenges and disappointments.

47. **Be patient when you ask your mother for something you need or want.** The process to acquire money/funds/resources takes time. What might seem simple for you may mean paying the mortgage/rent on time and buying the new big screen television you want for your room.

48. **Always tell your mother thank you.** No matter what, she tried and is always willing to try harder when she realizes how much you appreciate her efforts.

49. **Tell your mom the truth.** She cannot help you if you lie. She may not like what you did or how something happened, but she deserves the right

to know the truth. Trust me, mom's hate lie surprises.

50. **Respect your curfew.** Your safety is very important and it is not necessary to worry your mom. Call if you are going to be late. And do not make it a habit of being late.

SUPPLEMENTAL READING

PHYSICAL FITNESS & HEALTH

How to Eat to Live: Book One by Elijah Muhammad

The Power of Modesty: The Key to Health, Beauty & Longevity by Kevin A Muhammad (2010)

Natural Cures They Don't Want You to Know About by Kevin Trudeau (2004)

African Holistic Health by Laila Africa (1993)

SELF ESTEEM & SELF AWARENESS

Acts of Faith by Iyanla Vanzant (1993)

Daily Motivations for African American Success by Dennis Kimbro (1993)

Developing Positive Self Images and Discipline in Black Children by Jawanza Kunjufu (2000)

Real Love by Ava Muhammad (1999)

Superwomen & Goddesses by Akua Auset (2006)

Herstory: Black Females Rites of Passage by Mary Lewis (1988)

Fist, Stick, Knife Gun by Geoffrey Canada (1995)

CHAPTER BIBLIOGRAPHY

INTRODUCTION
Marriage in Black America. Retrieved July 5, 2014 from
http://blackdemographics.com/households/marriage-in-black-america/

Blacks struggle with 72 percent unwed mothers rate. Retrieved June 5, 2012 from
http://thegrio.com/2010/11/08/blacks-struggle-with-72-percent-unwed-mothers-rate/

A Teenage Girl Trafficked for Sex Tells Her Story. Retrieved November 5, 2014 from
http://www.essence.com/2009/10/26/a-teenage-girl-trafficked-for-sex-tells/

When Prisoners Return to the Community: Political, Economic, and Social Consequences. Petersilia, Joan (2010) Retrieved July 5, 2014 from
https://www.ncjrs.gov/pdffiles1/nij/184253.pdf

PERSONAL HYGEINE
Drinking Enough Water, WebMD. Retrieved July 5, 2014 from
http://www.webmd.com/a-to-z-guides/drinking-enough-water-topic-overview

Water: How much should you drink everyday? Retrieved July 5, 2014 from
http://www.cnn.com/HEALTH/library/water/NU00283.html

Expert Q&A: African-American Hair Care By Liesa Goins Retrieved July 5, 2014 from
http://www.webmd.com/beauty/hair-styling/expert-q-and-a-african-american-hair-care

Menstruation and the menstrual cycle fact sheet. Retrieved July 11, 2014 from http://www.womenshealth.gov/publications/our-publications/fact-sheet/menstruation.html

Dressing right to prevent yeast infections. Retrieved September 12, 2013 from http://www.everydayhealth.com/yeast-infection/clothing.aspx

Wearing tight jeans, skinny pants, spanx may be hazardous to your health. Retrieved August 10, 2013 from http://www.cbsnews.com/news/warning-tight-pants-skinny-jeans-and-spanx-may-be-hazardous-to-your-health/

EXERCISE & PHYSICAL FITNESS
Physical Activity Guidelines for Americans. Retrieved April 2014 from http://www.health.gov/PAGuidelines/

All about fasting for health and healing. Retrieved May 2014 from http://www.allaboutfasting.com/benefits-of-fasting.html

SELF-ESTEEM
Why Is Public Speaking Important? Retrieved July 12, 2014 from http://writingcommons.org/open-text/genres/public-speaking/844-why-is-public-speaking-important

SCHOOL
The Civil Rights Data Collection, Retrieved July 10, 2014 from http://ocrdata.ed.gov/

AROUND THE HOUSE LIFE SKILLS
Nutrition Information for you. Retrieved July 2013 from http://www.nutrition.gov/life-stages/adolescents/tweens-and-teens

Fast Meals & quick snacks: a cookbook for teens. Retrieved July 2014 from http://www.cdph.ca.gov/HealthInfo/healthyliving/childfamily/Documents/MO-NUPA-TeenCookbook.pdf

How To Clean Things Around The House, Retrieved July 12, 2014 from http://www.household-management-101.com/how-to-clean-things.html

ABOUT THE AUTHOR

Dr. Toni Sims-Muhammad has been teaching marriage and family for over 20 years and has taught at several institutions in the United States including Grambling State University, Georgia Perimeter College, Western Illinois University, University of Phoenix, and the University of Louisiana at Lafayette. She is a dynamic motivational independent scholar who's teaching, research and activism has inspired thousands. For more visit her website
http://www.tonisimsmuhammad.com.

CONTRIBUTORS

Tynetta Muhammad	Ava Muhammad
Dr. Jacqueline Dennis	Marva Muhammad
Nisa I. Muhammad	Majidah Muhammad

www.ingramcontent.com/pod-product-compliance
Lightning Source LLC
LaVergne TN
LVHW051058080426
835508LV00019B/1949